Manifestation. Accountability. Partner. Workbook

Co-Create The Life You Desire With The Universe

Life Goals Edition

ASHLEY

GUILLARD

ISBN: 978057883296-8

DEDICATION

Dedicated to freedom seekers all around the world.

This Workbook Belongs To:

Date:

Remarks:

CONTENTS

ACKNOWLEDGMENTS

Thank you to all who made this possible.

INTRODUCTION

One of the most important requirements of manifestation is to have a clear vision what you want. Having a clear knowing of your desires allows for the universe to create the atmosphere and opportunities that leads to the manifestation of your desires. Having a distorted view of your desires, puts you in the danger of existing in life aimlessly with no clear view of the future. This book, Manifestation. Accountability. Partner. Workbook helps you to overcome the barrier of intention setting by helping you organize and discover your desires. This enables you to set clear guidance for your manifestation partners (the universe and all of its counterparts). With this guide you'll be able to answer the most important manifestation question: What do I want?

The spiritual universe is your partner and this book is

your manifesto. A manifesto is the official document you and the universe use to co-create your desires. This helps you and the universe have a map or guide to where you are going. Think of it as a shared document used by you and your spiritual helpers to create your best life.

There are key manifestation factors in addition to the manifesto that is essential to making the partnership you have with the universe work. Proper understanding of these factors contributes to your ability to manifest the life you desire harmoniously. The essential factors are as follows:

Harm to None: This book isn't about manifesting people, places and things that cause undue harm. The instruction provided in this book is given with the presumption that your manifestations add value to your life and the world. It is possible to manifest things that cause harm. Therefore, if that is not your intent, it is important to profess that you'd like to manifest without causing harm to your people, places or things, as well as others. With this book, Manifestation. Accountability. Partner. Workbook, you manifest with the energy of love.

Faith: The partnership you have with the spirit of the universe requires faith. You may not have the ability to see how your requests will manifest. Therefore, you must trust that your spiritual partner has it covered. If you don't have faith in your spiritual partner, the partnership will not work, and it'll be more difficult to manifest your desires.

Timing: The timing on the manifestation of your desires depends on many factors that you may not fully understand. Therefore, it's best to do your part and trust in divine timing. However, rely on spiritual communication if you would like more information on when your manifestations will occur.

Communication: The universe has many tongues. Spiritual communication comes in the form of dreams, numerology, prophetic messages, animals, astrology, or a more direct approach like tarot readings from a spiritual advisor. If you are in the need of guidance or direction use one of those forms of communication to get guidance from the spirit of God that knows all and is all. From my experience, spirit gives prophecy and guidance. When I have a goal that requires my time, money and energy, I conduct a spiritual reading on it, to see what the spirit of higher knowledge has to say about the goal. For example, before continuing with this manifestation workbook series I did a reading on the potential return. That way, I could invest my time and energy wisely. If you want to know how to assist in the realization of your manifestations, there's a tarot reading for that. If you want a prediction as to when or how your manifestations will occur, there's a reading for that. If you'd like a tarot reading from me, email me at tarotbyashleyg@gmail.com or go to your trusted spiritual advisor.

Trust: Faith is similar to trust. However, trust is required when your faith is challenged. You may experience a life challenge that creates the false illusion that your desires aren't manifesting. During that experience it's important to remain in the energy of trust. Trust the process. Trust in divine timing. Trust that everything happens for a reason. Trust that regardless of what's occurring, your manifestations are coming into realization. Match your trust with action by continuing to work towards the fruition of your desires.

Strengths: The strength of the universe is unlimited. The universe is omnipotent (has unlimited power), omnipresent (present everywhere and connected to everything and everyone at the same time) & omniscient (knows everything). What an amazing partner to have! At any time, the spirit can move people to do things that'll assist you in your manifestations. If you need favor with a lender, school, institution, person, place or thing; the spirit of the universe has a person for that. Your strength is in your body, life and existence, giving the spirit a vessel to live through. Your strength is also in your connection to the spirit of God.

Weaknesses: The spirit of God and the universe has no weaknesses. Therefore, the control of weaknesses is all within you. A limited perception of the universe and it's capabilities are weaknesses. A limited perception of your reality is a weakness. Uncontrolled emotions are a weakness. The flesh can sometimes lead to weakness if it isn't used properly. By following the key manifestation factors, you'll be able to overcome or properly manage weaknesses.

Limitations: There are no limits with spirit. However, time may be perceived as a limitation to those who are too eager to trust in divine timing. I've been there, I understand. However, I've learned that everything happens for a reason in its due season.

Personal Accountability: You and the spirit of the universe are partners. Therefore, it's important to do your part. Your manifestations are an assignment. Your role is to follow the key factors and do what you physically can within your limitations. If there is something that needs to be done beyond your physical reach, your spiritual partner will help you.

How To Use This Book:

1. You don't have to fill it out in order. Go to the section you're currently manifesting.
2. It's okay to make changes as needed. It's a plan but plans get revised all the time.
3. You can manifest using pictures and/or words.
4. Follow up on your manifestations by communicating with your spiritual partner. You can do this in the form of spiritual communication of your choice.
5. Leave sections blank until you're clear about what you'd like to manifest in that area of your life.
6. Stay positive and in the energy of expectation. Especially while using this book, your manifestation tool.
7. Manifest in the energy of expectation and rest. Rest is an

uncompromising mindset that your manifestations are coming. It doesn't mean that you aren't working. It means your mind is at ease because you have complete confidence in yourself and your spiritual partner.

Sections:

The sections in the Life Goals Edition of the Manifestation. Accountability. Partner. Workbook work together to manifest the culmination of your life. It includes the following topics:

Manifest My World: We all share the world. However, each of us have our own individual experience as a result of what we are born into and what we create. This section comprises of your manifestations that together create your world. It is how you'd like to experience life. You can co-create your experience with the spirit of the universe, or you can let the outer environment create your experience for you.

This section includes ***immediate goals, lifestyle goals, home goals, location goals, financial goals, active income goals, passive income goals, credit goals, debt goals, material things, abundant life goals, friend goals and vacation goals.***

Manifest My Body: Your body is your temple. It is how you present yourself to the world. This section is about manifesting your outer appearance. It may seem vain but it's not. It's okay to work on your body until you love what you see. This section can cover anything body related. You can manifest your ***appearance, body confidence, health, eating habits, body performance, hair, skin & nails, style,*** or whatever you'd like with no judgement. This workbook is all about you and the life you want to experience. That includes surface level things.

Manifest My Mind: Your mind is a powerful part of you that many don't use to its capacity. Determine what you'd like to do with this power. How do you want to use your mind? You can manifest ***education, knowledge, mental liberation, expertise, different languages,*** and anything else you'd like to learn.

Manifest My Spirit: The spirit living inside of you is connected to the multiverse. It's the higher version of you. Many go their entire existence ignoring this part of them; never getting to experience life to its fullest. This is, in my opinion, the most important section to manifest because it opens the door for everything else and more. In this section you manifest ***more life, enlightenment, wisdom, emotional healing, spiritual wholeness, spiritual connection, spiritual protection, ancestral connection, and spell removal and protection***. If done with intent and purity, you'll manifest the transformation of your life.

Manifest Myself: The worlds distractions can get in the way of your knowledge of self. Sometimes people get lost in the worlds drama, the challenge of mere existence, their emotions, and in the people, places and things they place in their lives to mask the pain of not knowing themselves. This section is for those who want to manifest themselves. It covers ***self-love, personal evolution, emotional fulfillment, self-actualization, and the discovery of your life***.

Manifest My Kingdom: The Oxford definition of A kingdom is a territory ruled by a king or queen or the spiritual reign or authority of God. Your kingdom is your contribution to the advancement of the world. It's a cumulation of your creations. It is the value you add to the world and to those impacted by your world. When you manifest your spirit, you manifest your kingdom, your reign, your authority, and more. This section of the Manifestation. Accountability. Partner. Workbook covers your ***career, partner, relationships, legacy, family, assets, long-term wealth, brand, business, customers, products, services, community, and what you leave behind (your will)***.

Manifest My Increase: Growth never ends.

Abundance never ends. Once abundance manifests it continuously grows in its due seasons. This section is for your creations. The ideas and things that you'll manifest in the short or long-term future, to ensure the continuous growth of yourself and your kingdom. It covers ideas that'll take you to the ***next level, visions and channeled thoughts.***

Manifest Anything: At the end of the workbook there is space for you to ***manifest anything*** that may not be covered in the other sections. There is also space for ***notes*** and ***monthly manifestations***.

Remember, as you begin and continue the manifestation process, the spirit of the universe will introduce people, places and things in your life that'll lead to the manifestation of your desires. Due to human nature, this process isn't always comfortable. People, places and things that are hindrances to your process are at risk of being removed from your life. If you hold on to hindrances, it slows down your manifestation process. However, your spiritual partner will help you remove them from your life comfortably or not. I wish you many blessings on your journey to more life and freedom. Leave your limitations at the door.

When you're partners with the universe, you can create anything. All is possible for you.

AFFIRMATIONS

I decree & declare that I have a partnership with the universal Spirit of God that assists me with manifesting the desires of my heart, with no harm to none. Mote it be, it is done, Amen.

Start your manifestation process by declaring and affirming who you are and the life you want to live.

MANIFEST MY WORLD

IMMEDIATE GOALS

Your spiritual partner, the universe and it's counterparts, are rarely in a rush. However, sometimes humans are. Especially when the seeds planted yesterday, or lack thereof, hasn't manifested the harvest needed to survive comfortably. This leads to the perception of lack. To overcome this perceived lack, ask the universe to manifest your immediate desires that allows for a peaceful manifestation process. What do you need to live physiologically, psychologically and for safety?

LIFESTYLE GOALS

Your lifestyle is your way or style of living. Once you know how you want to experience life, you'll know how much money you need to make it happen. How do you want to experience life? Use words or pictures to set the vision for you and your spiritual partner. Manifest your desired lifestyle. If you could imagine your life into existence what would it be?

HOME GOALS

Your home is your place of peace. Use this section to manifest your dream home, your next home, or both. Manifest the energy of your home, its ambience, appearance, the presence of your home, how you'd like visitors to feel in your home, neighbors, characteristics, neighborhood, community and aesthetics.

LOCATION GOALS

Weather, culture, education, environment, people, support, and your kingdom are some of the things to consider when choosing where you want to reside. Where will you make your mark?

FINANCIAL GOALS

The amount of money you make has influence over the life you live. Considering your lifestyle goals, how much do you need to make? This section goes over how much money you'd like to make. The next sections go over how you'd like to get it. If you'd like to be practical you can set steppingstones as you progress towards your overall financial goal. Small accomplishments add up to major accomplishments.

ACTIVE INCOME GOALS

Active income is how you participate in the manifestation of financial increase. Manifest how you'd like to actively earn income. You can list activities, products, services, or you can be vague.

PASSIVE INCOME GOALS

The body has limitations. To overcome the physical limitations of the body, manifest passive ways to earn money. You don't have to work yourself to your physical limits to increase financially. You can earn money in your sleep, on vacation, and more. Partner with people, places and things that earn money for and with you.

CREDIT GOALS

Leverage your credit to create your lifestyle and to build your kingdom. Use this section to work towards and manifest credit building, restoration and your desired score. The goal is to be positioned to partner with those who can assist in the manifestation of your world and kingdom. Good credit presents you as a reliable partner.

DEBT GOALS

Good debt makes you rich. Bad debt works against your riches. Manifest the erasure or repayment of bad debt. Manifest the creation of good debt. Manifest good financial partners and fair contracts.

MATERIAL THINGS

Things bring us temporary joy. Use this section to manifest the things that will add value to your world, kingdom and life experience.

ABUNDANT LIFE

You can manifest money, a lifestyle, home, vehicles and things. However, none of that erases unhappiness. Having an abundant life includes happiness, peace, love, gratitude, appreciation, connections and more. Manifest what would make your existence abundant.

FRIEND GOALS

Your friends are who you choose to share your life with. They make moments more enjoyable and memories worth smiling over. Manifest your support group of friends and their qualities. Manifest who you'd like to be as a friend.

VACATION GOALS

While you're in the world you might as well enjoy and experience it. What places would you like to see? How would you like to experience your vacations? How would you like to travel? Use this space to manifest your dream travel experiences.

MANIFEST MY BODY

APPEARANCE

Are you happy with your appearance? If not it's okay. Make the changes you'd like to make and learn to love the changes you can't. Use pictures and words to manifest your appearance.

BODY CONFIDENCE

Body confidence is about loving your body even if the wickedness of the world has trained you not to. People are programmed from birth. That includes faulty programs that train people to like certain attributes and dislike others. If you are the aesthetic look the world is taught to love, that's great. Love yourself regardless. If you aren't, you're great too. Love yourself regardless.

HEALTH GOALS

A healthy body, mind and spirit is essential to living life to the fullest. Manifest the continuation of good health throughout your life journey. If you'd like, you may also profess your desired life expectancy and how you'd like to look and function during your older ages.

EATING HABITS

Be careful of the things you put into your body. Especially if you want it to last and be vibrant for 80 or more years. Use this space to manifest good eating habits and to learn what's best to fuel your body.

BODY PERFORMANCE

Many athletes and physically fit people have taken their bodies places that the average person hasn't. I've always been intrigued by people who can do gymnastics, professionally swim, run fast, stretch beyond the norm, do power yoga, grow muscles, or anything that pushes their bodies beyond the average performance. If you want to be a part of this elite group of people use this section to begin the process of using your body to its maximum capacity.

HAIR, SKIN & NAILS

This space is to manifest the changes you'd like to make to your hair, skin and nails. It's also to manifest health corrections that impact these areas.

STYLE

Your style is your outward expression of who you are and how you feel. It is also what others process to create their perception of you. What story do you want to tell with your style? Use this space to create the story you want to tell others with your style. Use words and pictures if you'd like to.

MANIFEST
MY
MIND

EDUCATION

Manifest your desired field of study and or any areas of expertise you'd like to master. What would you like to be the answer to that requires a formal education?

KNOWLEDGE

Self-knowledge is key to freeing your mind. When you self-teach, unlearn faulty programs, and relearn key information, you free yourself from faulty programming. Use this section to manifest knowledge.

MENTAL LIBERATION

Unlearn faulty programming. You may be unaware of the misinformation you've been taught. Therefore, manifesting mental liberation is asking the universe to free your mind from the bondage of the enemy that may be keeping you ignorant, uninformed or ill informed. Use this space to request the spirit of the universe to free your mind. Write what you've learned.

EXPERTISE

What would you like to be the subject matter expert of? For example, I have a master's degree in Human Resources Management (HRM). I worked in Federal HR and there were several disciplines that I could've mastered: Recruitment & Placement, Classification, HR Systems, or any other area. Use this section to manifest subject matter expertise in your desired field.

LANGUAGES

Use this space to set the intention of learning other languages that you desire. For example, coding or Hebrew, French, Spanish or any other language you prefer.

MANIFEST
MY
SPIRIT

MORE LIFE

The enemy comes to steal, kill and destroy: I AM comes so that they might have life, and that they may have it abundantly (John 10:10 KJV). Manifesting more life is an invitation to enhance your life experience by becoming one with the spirit of God living inside of you. It's not about religion but about life and becoming one with the spirit of the universe. Religion, spiritual practices or a spiritual journey, if done properly, leads you there. Use this section to manifest more life. You can write God's promises, or a simple date and request asking the spirit of God to live through you. Manifest it as you please.

ENLIGHTENMENT

To enlighten is to have greater knowledge or understanding about life. Spiritual enlightenment allows you to tap into spiritual knowledge that knows all. Manifest enlightenment if you'd like to have a greater understanding of spiritual matters, life and the world.

WISDOM

You grow in wisdom when you've acquired experience in life and grow spiritually. To manifest wisdom you're asking the spirit of the universe to introduce people, places, things and experiences to your life that you'll grow from. Use this space to manifest wisdom.

EMOTIONAL HEALING

The culmination of your higher self, calls for the healing and release of emotional baggage. What's holding you back from your elevation? Manifest emotional healing. Use this as a safe space to heal from emotional trauma. Your higher self depends on it.

SPIRITUAL WHOLENESS

This section is for people who'd like to be one with the dualities of themselves. Body, spirit and creator as one. It's very similar to more life but more about you becoming whole, forgiven and reconnected to the creator. More life is the result of you being whole.

SPIRITUAL CONNECTION

This section is for people who desire to be spiritual practitioners, mediums, tarot card readers, spiritual leaders and for people who want to connect to the spirit realm. If you'd like to have a spiritual connection that allows for you to work with the spirit of the universe, to help yourself and others; use this space to manifest that.

SPIRITUAL PROTECTION

For spiritual protection speak *Psalm 91* into your life. This isn't about religion it's a request to manifest spiritual protection. I break down each scripture below and put it into spiritual context and clarity.

Psalm 91 KJV:

1 Whoever dwells in the shelter of the Most High will rest in the shadow of the Almighty.

- Whoever connects with the spirit of God inside of them will be protected by the creator.

2 ..."He is my refuge and my fortress, my God, in whom I trust."

- The spirit of God protects you and keeps you safe, have

complete trust in it.

3 Surely, he will save you from the fowler's snare and from the deadly pestilence.

- Your spiritual connection will keep you safe from the evils of the world.

4 He will cover you with his feathers, and under his wings you will find refuge; his faithfulness will be your shield and rampart.

- You will be hidden from the enemy.

5 You will not fear the terror of night, nor the arrow that flies
by day, 6 nor the pestilence that stalks in the darkness, nor
the plague that destroys at midday.

- You'll be protected from all kinds of evil.

7 A thousand may fall at your side, ten thousand at your right hand, but it will not come near you.

- There will be people who aren't protected by the spirit of God from evil and they will fall but because of your partnership with the spirit of God, evil will not come near you, regardless of what's happening to them.

8 You will only observe with your eyes and see the punishment of the wicked.

- Though you'll be protected you'll see the evil happening in the world.

9 If you say, "The Lord is my refuge," and you make the Most High your dwelling, 10 no harm will overtake you; no disaster will come near your tent.

- If you request spiritual protection and be one with the spirit of God living inside of you, no harm will overtake you, no disaster will come near you.

11 For he will command his angels concerning you to guard you in all your ways; 12 they will lift you up in their hands, so

that you will not strike your foot against a stone.

- God's Angels will protect you.

13 You will tread on the lion and the cobra; you will trample the great lion and the serpent.

- Animals will protect you.

14 "Because you love me, I will rescue you; I will protect you, for you acknowledges my name."

- Because you know the Spirit of God and It's power you'll be rescued from evil.

15 You will call on me, and I will answer you; I will be with you in trouble, I will deliver you and honor you.

- If you need help, all you'll have to do is ask. The spirit of God will honor your request.

16 "With long life I will satisfy you and show you my salvation."

- You'll be blessed with more life, forgiveness and freedom.

Use this space to manifest spiritual protection.

ANCESTRAL CONNECTION

My ancestors visit me in dreams. They teach me lessons, talk to me, bless me, protect me and guide me. They've even told me when to play the lottery. Although I miss my grandmother's physical presence, I feel closer to her in spirit. I also have connections to my soul tribe and spiritual ancestors through heritage; alive and dead. If you'd like to be connected to your ancestors and soul tribe, use this space to manifest it. Write the intuitive requests that come to you.

SPELL REMOVAL & PROTECTION

No weapons formed against you shall prosper. Every tongue that accuses you in judgment you will condemn (Isaiah 54:17). Use this space to request awareness of negative spells you're influenced by and to manifest protection against spells and ill will plotted against you.

MANIFEST MYSELF

SELF LOVE

Before you can properly love someone else, without being codependent, toxic or using them as a distraction to your lack of self-worth, you must learn to love yourself. It may require you to unlearn the experiences, habits and messages that created a mental environment of self-hate (or a faulty self-esteem). Maybe you love yourself but could use a booster. Use this space to manifest self-love and self-respect. What do you want to love about yourself?

PERSONAL EVOLUTION

Remember who you are. To manifest personal evolution is to radically accept who you are and your purpose in life. It is to create the space for growth in all areas of your existence and to become who you would like to be. Use this space to manifest personal evolution.

EMOTIONAL FULFILLMENT

Inner and external love, a love of life, connections, friendship, intimacy, esteem, family, a feeling of accomplishment, and a feeling of importance are aspects of your life that leads to emotional fulfillment. Use this space to manifest a life experience that fulfills you.

SELF ACTUALIZATION

Self actualization is a desire to become the absolute best person you can be. It brings admiration and respect from others. It also includes influence, recognition, fame, strength, power and freedom. Use this space to manifest self-actualization.

DISCOVERY OF LIFE

I don’t want to call it a “bucket list” so I’ll call it a life list. Use this area to manifest life enjoyment and experiences. What would you like to experience while you're here in the physical?

MANIFEST
MY
KINGDOM

CAREER GOALS

What work would you like to do? Manifest your job description, how much you'd like to make, your position, the stakeholders, the culture, environment, desired organization and more.

PARTNER GOALS

Your partner builds your kingdom with you. What desires do you have in a partner? Who do you want as a co-partner to build and manage your kingdom with? Use this space to manifest desired characteristics, attributes, and anything you desire in a partner.

RELATIONSHIP GOALS

No successful kingdom runs alone. The rulers of kingdoms have relationships with people in all areas of their lives to grow and maintain it. Additionally, a fulfilling life is enhanced by connections. Many people lose connections with people from their past as they grow. Use this space to manifest mutually beneficial, fulfilling and genuine connections.

LEGACY

What if what and who you leave behind returns to you in your next lifetime? Use this space to clarify your legacy intentions with the spirit of the universe. Your legacy is what you leave behind, how you're remembered and how you made others feel.

FAMILY

Your family is an important part of your kingdom. They help to manifest your kingdom and enjoy it with you. Your family may also be responsible for the continuation of your kingdom. Use this space to manifest good things for your family if you desire.

ASSET GOALS

What assets would you like to acquire and how would you like to acquire them? You may also manifest the deals you'd like to get, and the results of the negotiations. What assets do you desire? For what purpose?

LONG-TERM WEALTH

Manifest long term wealth, assets and opportunities. How would you like your kingdom to create long-term wealth? Who or what organizations do you want to pay you on a long-term basis? What is the reason that they'll pay you long term?

BRAND GOALS

When people think of your brand what do you want them to think? Manifest your brand's perception, identity, mission, affiliates and other aspect of your brand.

BUSINESS GOALS

Manifest the business opportunities you'd like to create, manage or any business related goal that you'd like the Spirit of God to help you manifest into reality.

CUSTOMER GOALS

There's a group of people who will be willing to buy your products and services at your price point. Manifest the customer base that'll make your business and brand a success. How will you add value to their lives?

PRODUCT GOALS

Manifest the products you would like to create. Use this space for product creation inspiration. What products are you inspired to create? What do you need to create them?

SERVICE GOALS

Manifest the services you would like to create. Use this space for service creation inspiration. What service would you like offer or be a part of? What resources do you need to offer it?

COMMUNITY GOALS

Self-actualization comes with a tribe. The spiritual union with divine energies manifests you into a "fisher of humans". This results in you having a community of people that follow you, your gift, your brand, your business and your life. They are inspired by your life. They're a part of your legacy. Use this space to manifest your community. Who are they? How do you add value to their lives? How do you help them evolve? How do they help you?

WILLED INHERITANCE

Some people come into the world and leave their loved ones with a bill. What physical possessions do you want to leave? What impact do you want to have had on the lives of those you loved and connected with? Use this space to manifest your will and testament. Of course, this isn't a legal document, but it will help to manifest your intentions.

MANIFEST MY INCREASE

NEXT LEVEL

It's levels to financial security and it's levels to life. Use this space to manifest the next level in life, love, finances, career or any area of life that you're ready to advance in.

VISIONS

Your vision is your ability to think, plan and strategize your future. List your visions that have potential to manifest increase.

CHANNELED THOUGHTS

Communication is key to a successful partnership with the spirit of the universe. Use this space to decipher spiritual codes from spirit. Remember communication may be from dreams, a tarot reading, a prophet, a line in a movie that catches your attention, a sermon, or through anyone because we are all connected to the spirit of the universe.

MANIFEST ANYTHING

MANIFEST ANYTHING

Use this as a creative space to manifest anything you want. The manifestations that lead to an abundant life are covered in this book. However, use this space to think beyond what this workbook has to offer. What would you like to manifest?

JANUARY GOALS

Use this space to manifest your monthly objectives and goals. It also makes sense to list practical things. Your partnership with spirit manifests the spiritual and the practical.

FEBRUARY GOALS

Use this space to manifest your monthly objectives and goals. It also makes sense to list practical things. Your partnership with spirit manifests the spiritual and the practical.

MARCH GOALS

Use this space to manifest your monthly objectives and goals. It also makes sense to list practical things. Your partnership with spirit manifests the spiritual and the practical.

APRIL GOALS

Use this space to manifest your monthly objectives and goals. It also makes sense to list practical things. Your partnership with spirit manifests the spiritual and the practical.

MAY GOALS

Use this space to manifest your monthly objectives and goals. It also makes sense to list practical things. Your partnership with spirit manifests the spiritual and the practical.

JUNE GOALS

Use this space to manifest your monthly objectives and goals. It also makes sense to list practical things. Your partnership with spirit manifests the spiritual and the practical.

JULY GOALS

Use this space to manifest your monthly objectives and goals. It also makes sense to list practical things. Your partnership with spirit manifests the spiritual and the practical.

AUGUST GOALS

Use this space to manifest your monthly objectives and goals. It also makes sense to list practical things. Your partnership with spirit manifests the spiritual and the practical.

SEPTEMBER GOALS

Use this space to manifest your monthly objectives and goals. It also makes sense to list practical things. Your partnership with spirit manifests the spiritual and the practical.

OCTOBER GOALS

Use this space to manifest your monthly objectives and goals. It also makes sense to list practical things. Your partnership with spirit manifests the spiritual and the practical.

NOVEMBER GOALS

Use this space to manifest your monthly objectives and goals. It also makes sense to list practical things. Your partnership with spirit manifests the spiritual and the practical.

DECEMBER GOALS

Use this space to manifest your monthly objectives and goals. It also makes sense to list practical things. Your partnership with spirit manifests the spiritual and the practical.

MANIFESTATION BLOG, RESULTS & NOTES

ABOUT THE AUTHOR:

Ashley Guillard, a Chicago native, is a Spiritual Leader, a serial entrepreneur, and the author of numerous books to include, *DR3AM: The Spiritual Pathway to Success*, *Business Strategy Journal: A Step by Step Guide to A Successful Business Plan & Strategy, The Personification of Beauty, The Power of I AM, The War on Your Money, and* the *Manifestation., Accountability. Partner. Workbook Series.* She is also a Combat Veteran of the United States Army, member of Alpha Kappa Alpha Sorority, Inc., and the mother of Lamar Guillard, Jr. As a purpose driven millennial, Ashley is widely known for her passion for encouraging people to pursue excellence and to become the person they are called to be.

For More Information:

Email: TAROTBYASHLEYG@gmail.com

Website: www.AshleyGuillard.com

TikTok: Ashley Guillard

Instagram: @AshIsGod_

Made in the USA
Las Vegas, NV
03 January 2023